Ephemeris

Ephemeris

Dorothy Lehane

ISBN: 978-0-9927589-6-7

Copyright © Dorothy Lehane, 2014

Cover photograph © Eleanor Bennett
www.eleanorleonnebennett.zenfolio.com

All rights reserved. No part of this work may be reproduced, stored or transmitted in any form or by any means, graphic, electronic, recorded or mechanical, without the prior written permission of the publisher.

Dorothy Lehane has asserted her right under Section 77 of the Copyright, Designs and Patents Act 1988 to be identified as the author of this work.

First published October 2014 by:

Nine Arches Press
PO Box 6269
Rugby
CV21 9NL

www.ninearchespress.com

Printed in Britain by:

imprintdigital.net
Seychelles Farm,
Upton Pyne,
Exeter
EX5 5HY
www.imprintdigital.net

Ephemeris

Dorothy Lehane

Nine
Arches
Press

Debut
new poets series

Dorothy Lehane is an Assistant Lecturer in Creative Writing and PhD candidate in Poetry: Text Practice as Research at the University of Kent. Her research explores the perceptual and social experiences of neurological speech conditions, and examines questions concerning cultural encounters and embodied responses within poetic practice. Her chapbook *Places of Articulation* is forthcoming in November 2014 with dancing girl press, Chicago. She is the founding editor of Litmus Publishing, an Arts Council England funded press exploring the intersection of poetry and science. Her work has recently appeared in *Glasgow Review of Books, HARTS & Minds, Tears in the Fence,* and *Zone Magazine*. She has performed her work at various venues in the UK including The Barbican, The Science Museum, The Roundhouse, BBC Radio Kent, Sounds New Music Festival, In The Woods Festival and Canterbury Art Festival. *Ephemeris* is her debut collection of poems.

CONTENTS

STROMEN	11
Buckminster Fuller	12
Supernova	13
Unnova	14
Keyhole (NGC1999)	15
The Forces	16
Collison	19
Cosmic Rays	20
Phobos	21
Vintage	22
Einstein-Rosen Bridges	23
Goldilocks Zone	24
dark heart	25
Music of the Spheres	26
NGC 7317 (Stephan's Quintet)	27
Dimensions	28
Collider	30
Black Hole	31
Crab Nebula	32
ever after	33
Jewel Box	34
In Just One Sense	35
Reader	36
Hunters	37
Pulsar	38
the late heavy bombardment	39
Coronal Mass Ejection	40
Origins	41
Siamese	42
For Rebecca Elson	43
Coma Cluster	44
assemblage	45

collapsus	46
Moon	47
Sombrero galaxy	48
Distant Cousins	49
Merger	51
Das Medusenhaupt	52
Ring Nebula	53
Solidarity	55
Laika	56
Mirror	57
the interval proper to the idyll	58
Reanimate	59
Mimicry	60
Sonnet	61
Acknowledgements	63

for Mark

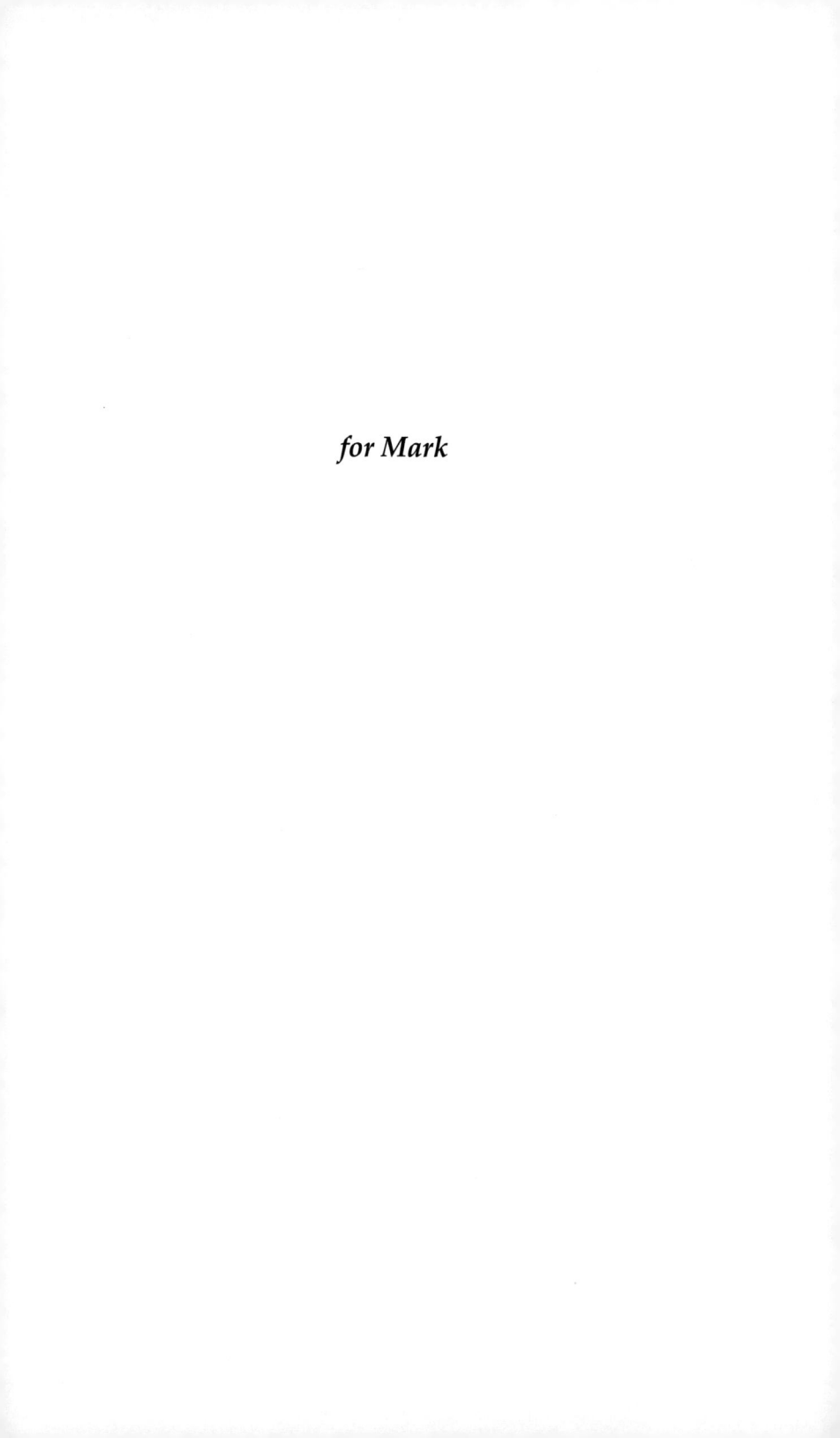

I live on Earth at present, and I don't know what I am. I know that I am not a category. I am not a thing – a noun. I seem to be a verb, an evolutionary process – an integral function of the universe.

Buckminster Fuller

Ephemeris (ĭfe·mĕris). pl. **ephemerides** (efĭme·ridĭz), formerly used as *sing.* 1551
† 1. A diary, journal - 1682.
2. A table showing the computed (rarely the observed) places of a heavenly body for every day of a given period. † Also, in *pl.* the tabulated positions of a heavenly body for a series of successive days 1551.
† **b.** *pl.* A collection of such tables - 1625
3. A book giving the places of the planets and other astronomical matters in advance for each day of a certain period; an astronomical almanac 1647.
† 4. An almanac or calendar of any kind. (Used in bibliographical works, in *pl.*, as a general heading for Almanacs, Calendars, etc.) - 1796.
5. ¶. *catachr* = EPHEMERA 1820. Honour is venerable to us because it is no e. EMERSON. Hence **Ephemerist,** one who makes or uses an e.

Oxford English Dictionary

STROMEN

begin with STROMEN for what it means to be human
as *good enough mother*
as early aphasiologists think
influx because there is no formulaic STROMEN
sing verbs as STROMENTS
you could say that a talking therapy cannot touch this
forcing itself into my purview
shedding avoirdupois
perfect unutterable castration of
blinded by my own STROMEN
arguing about leaving iron scrap out for the travellers
each poem ends with a solo
– do you know how complex iron fusion is
etc etc

Buckminster Fuller

heck, pioneer, maverick
Buckminsterfullerene: clean coal,
giant trilby, the dome geodosic

spacer molecules
unitary air is in the air

primitive bacteria are alive with you
man is not consciously cell
nor quasi-paradox

consumption with depression
meaning inertia

Supernova

worrying little striptease
soliloquise through the night
Liebestod blares through vestiges
sonic rolls a hormonal burst
we are a dying swarm
epilogue is epilogue is free carbon fade
reign the exotic dead
we couldn't make such colours
in an abattoir, garner or expel
choice is a bouquet
embryo is a sliding ache
a sort of emergency end
sure, bring on the dancing girls

Unnova

hidden in plain sight
elusive wink out / inside out
javeline flash
bloated turbulent envelope
elastic gas seems
a phenomena
compared to the quiet
ironing board
the chrome leg isn't bright
isn't looping polyphonies
percolating hailstones
local funeral / just going out

Keyhole (NGC1999)

       isn't exactly grown yet
barely sagacious
smashing freedom from cradles
malapert, oh, belligerent footholds
screw off baby tempests

how this happens is unclear
surge&speed   spit&charge

to erupt is a domination
an alpha male corralling cloud
vandals graffiti like a mirror
scattering culprits
metropolis in their jets

The Forces

$F = H * \exp(\frac{-s}{r_0})/s^2 [strong]$

unwaged intent, l'enfant terrible will implode,
Judy Garland seismograph, Richter rotatory teal,
milk of the poppy, F4 Tornado, homeland security,
cowboy, no isms, ruptures, fortify my transgressions;
military secrets, uranium, legal leviathan, axon & vomit,
polaroid dementia, quench all impetus. We are out
of superlatives, amyl nitrate, threshing vehement,
think bone infection, Bikini Atoll, the whole side issue,
cruel antique, assemble your best men, this cavity
is sizeable, take additives, shake and cover

$F(em) = k.Q. \frac{q}{r^2} [weak]$

you are touching my particles
parents included, splinters, survivors of imperatives,
it's a frisson, just flying round, disorganised, bones,
and sparks. I think you are definitely just going to be
a friend, insouciant in bed, it's the slip of baptism,
shedding toxic paint, I hitched home without using
my fucking thumb, without song, there goes another night,
uprooted, and sealed like a scar bursting, a haematoma,
or zip catching and re-sealing, let's not abandon it here,
we should write it, make plans for next week,
for cleavage, for sleeping rough, for fracas –

$$F = q(E + v + B)[electro]$$

twelve torrential hours to run, to turn philosopher,
transpose lovers, excel commando, antibiotic pin-up girl,
forget tea in lieu of Glenfiddich, high-class chatterbox
no time for libidinous dream, this is night-scape,
there are no vitamins for this, no auspices,
for salicylic acid, leave marigolds inside out,
birds fly with rhapsodic clatter, swoop below thermals
thunder heads clash, cloud anvil ribbon re-strike,
staccato lightning, we have lost all mating calls,
the earth is fried, immaculate, bedecked in ashes,
demise & swirl, take the monorail, ride out the city,
out of the maw-maw office, throwaway homes,
  throwaway graves

$$Fg = \frac{Gm^1 m^2}{r^2} [gravity]$$

made up by science; same evolution,
same dinosaurs, same helix cheeky tryptic,
de facto damn, *tsk* gravity, blame recreational sex,
Galileo Galilei is a pal of tall order,
we are talking torsion, postulations, telekinesis,
who has been invited to our pool party,
masquerade only, call gravity clotted,
if a clot is a mass and if a mass falls,
warfarin combats that, seafaring combats echo,
better than dying in a vacuum,
anticoagulant is a dignified lapse,
we won't use balloons in examples,

certainly can't use feather-care.
parachutists: if only harmonics would govern them,
relic pins in legs, unfastening guts,
impaling, avionic collage,
I am pretty sure our contingency for primal film
should be set in anti-gravity, inertial conditions,
with a dog floating unequivocally, because somehow
a canine is funny,
     thanks then for gravity,
if you think about urine floating,
certainly the repose is *thanks*

Collision

at first surge, love:
galaxy meet galaxy, gestalt smile
for compression waves
thunder-heads; silly little novas
elemental cheese in bed
whacked out maelstrom fights
the masses with fireworks
we have alibis – justified smears
politics by emblematic wing
flanked by fragrance, collect coupons
try a midnight stagger, assimilate
like speech-monkeys; skin, the love-treaty
merge to silence, self-hood hell-bent
missing an axis, recovery nucleus
cartwheel, sort of rushing
spells, lexis, praxis, gridlocked
in fraud, lust is that trick, verify
guesswork, rip out stagnation

Cosmic Rays

hold up cosmic ray
  pure niche, bombarding
   in relentless droves
    wallop by wallop
     lousy low energy
      if the zodiac is coming
       if I untangle your tangled hair
       wipe away cosmic spittle
        romance is a lethal stripper
        gamma rays for each
        of my old lovers
         one poem per day
          for each of my cats
           my cat would love to slit
            my throat, my old lovers
           would love to watch
          eat porridge
              granular bars akimbo

Phobos

they may call you aspergic,
statement you, beautiful vacuous child,
sweet old surd, give tapestry answers,
empty eyes, hung-up wasteland atmosphere,
hollow conglomerate, what is this façade,
lo, from which contingent? What hell-bent
question mark lurks over you, love handle
or lore, equatorial hanger-on huh huh habitat,
siesta until the sun rises, no ball games now

Vintage

White dwarfs encumbered by aged bodies. Here and now. *Appellation Contrôlée*; Reblochon, Pinot Noir, Yellowism. Core collapsing, barbiturates in pillboxes; everything learnt into a compressed philosophy, blue menopause, diamond judgement, no one likes a jaunty soundtrack. Crystallised rue, dementia is luminous: look away if you want retinal survival, go cubic lattice, yes.

Sea of electron, hop – exploit, satellites rank senility in stuttering flanks; we are truly irritable, crosswords – iron brain exercise if we believe it. We are uncanny survivors manoeuvrings this way that way. Gestural world. Teeth, formaldehyde. A nexus of new bone marrow. Call this necromancy, no, call this *standard model*. Sullen froth. All aesthete will end. What's left behind. Oh yes, we have words for all this.

Ligaments, strong ways, gummy pavement palette. Stubbed out subsidence, hankie spit, artichoke is a veg, is a fruit, tomato is a veg, is a fruit, first pronouns by church lychgates, confetti base, until the widows pause, smoke hard, crush against, pant, perfect axle fingers rising up, restart a route, end a tenure right there. We disinfect dead husbands, spend such little time in the mirror.

Einstein-Rosen Bridges

Reluctant rubber sheets
        ghost fold, tribal zealots in full weave

             register this worm
      plumb secrets into lost rivers
cry airborne kink

jump through English summer
afflicted thumbs up, disgorged space time
        ethereal flow, ethereal buttons

        mucky intestine trellis.

Mississippi Delta, effluent liver lake
gut of worm   butcher ancient dimensions
bankrupt umbilicus

have we spoken about time's vortex at all?
        too small to slide light through
slip humans into the middle ear;
ultimate diaspora   *weeeeeeee*   what a pivot

the dream is to flee, stoic flight
unbearable hiss,   this noise is the noise
of another childhood

Goldilocks Zone

Not too hot, not too cold, but just right.
  Robert Southey

Meet you on Titan,
lex loci, take a lifeboat
    as the red giant bloats
luminary & exhausted

we call safe haven
the big engulfing
human sterility is a no-no

deep freeze mother
primordial grime
    don't speak now, hypoglycaemics.
Titan, shrugging freeze
trigger clement
meet you on the hillside
say *what a small new world*
don't say *toska*
    toska won't cover this.

dark heart

dark heart/white bloom
swathes of gas
cloaked in a blinding fog

over the celestial Rubicon
poised to crush
leave me to singularity
leave me to join this new dimension

on the underground
two women sign to each other
Makaton in their mouths
bodies full instrument
deconstructing code

we, the carriage
silent like understudies
deaf in the wings
or swallowed, as though
all relevance has been sucked out

Music of the Spheres

instruments for the ear
        consonants of hammers
                the weight of hammers, dog hammers
gut strings, plucky experiments, perfect fourth perfect fifth

maths and harmonies in the macro/micro
hammers and anvils in the exo/oxo

can you hear that, sweet heptatonic prima
our chain of perfect fifths, back-street octaves
we say no worries but oh   yes, we have worries

chink each cluster of crystal, chink each Kir Royal
chink Plato's dialogues,   *shhh* the cosmos is singing
a seductress in harmony   in coherence   in design

whistling planets, in our ears since birth
                hey nubile soundtrack
high note, oh heck, fixed star, low note
        oh hell, moon if you like

Ptolemy's harmony
        seven planets   seven thoughts   seven states
your song lingers in my body
stretches from the turbulence
        of each supermarket twang twang
        the planets chime
bring that model perfect model

NGC 7317 (Stephan's Quintet)

Limb by limb, legless, kiss me combatant, are we brothers or are we bastards, bystanding is a sin for the fey. Sneaky loggerheads, bitter-Sodom-whacked-out-Gomorrah, at each juncture criminal, how they audio prowl under your skin, hot-headed, surviving. Move out siblings, bystanders are the ones to watch; slitting throats as you sleep, mode one: down&out, mode two: fair duelling. NGC7317: Sub human, forget human, you are a spurious agent, hooded pretence, masquerading on the outskirts as only a trickster inflates. *Wars, the horrors of mothers.* You are gossiping, neutrino by neutrino, straight through human skin, your pulp has power of attorney over my pulp, wear brogues or Doc Martens, brothers never explain kickback, how air-rifles *cha-yak cha-yak*, which brotherhood is the correct logarithm, which brother denies proximity, shoots pylons with laser fingers, role-plays history: Pearl Harbour, Purple Hearts, Hiroshima will happen when Dad ignites the engine.

Dimensions

We haven't said enough of the third dimension;
concealing its neighbours from us
how we grow regardless, lancing incisors
showing breast, mapping sweet epigrams
in this dimension, you tell me the genesis
of your name, oh, lord of Ireland, from stardust
or bombshell, you might see me in essence
watching the drunks in the pub opposite
if it is really, really late a commuter
walking home; irregular feet for drink
regular feet for ambition

      in a sixth dimension, I am a girlfriend
breathing fire, long hair pointy face, kicked out
from a black hole, in this dimension
we are the sixth universe; January through June,
five careful kernels in the library, you tell me
in this dimension, I am your wife; your third wife
reading poems your first wife hated, much less like you
and your second wife, how, in this poem
I am also android and how, absolutely
like your current wife, or that in-between Virgo
in this dimension, for certain we are involved
in something

      You and I held captive in the ninth dimension;
here before us, watching the flames
spit with a burned refractory, lichen, granite
glassy sand. Over your shoulder shouting a final
post-script, out of earshot, a sick unsound
and you are a missing, leaving a lingering chroma,
motes of dust scattered in the air, like a wrap
of skin cells from cushion chairs in a village hall
after a talk on ornithology

Collider

      Thief; beauty in the eye
pull wool over   eye to beholder
sarcoma eye
so much for hubbub bub
      this is the true spin-down, parched
      uttermost star-quake

crochet at a low ebb
      you can have one vignette over the eight
a Dutch tilt for antiques, balsam the electroweak
size of an apple, mass of a jungle or Earth
      we can hide inside glueballs or gluons
hit hard in the quark-gluon plasma, if we need to revive
gluey vision or hot universes
post mortem finds one existing betamax

are you gamma bursts or Q stars
intent on carrying me across the threshold
or will I balter across the room
gorse in my hair?

Ask yourself which you'll recreate;
      isospin, strangeness, charm
see you in a kudocast
since you are wondering
      walla walla   *walla walla*

Black Hole

Soviet art; matador or assassin
high kick/low kick
map something progressive:
    trails of pebbles,
plasma and cellular fluid riding,
spinning like   rotors or drunks,
swallowing lapsang, opera,
fetish. Backwards,
already unpredictable;
verbal jets to nucleic acid,

nothing like a worry, nothing
like a solar system, or liver shifting,

also a counterbalance,

in the middle of it all; jaundiced,
feverish,   holding baby teeth
in the palm of her hand:
I kept your teeth,   little epochs,
bygone rocks, clays,
fool's gold   sulphides,

I am thinking of rhubarb –
how rhubarb will destroy everything.

Crab Nebula

Haven't we been through this:
stellar cinders in AD 1054,
corpse pervading with new engine isotopes
decayed but forging still;
unlikely Lazarus, celestial zombie
Speak-easy dynamo, forge anew:
nature abhors a vacuum,
islands, scale, high-point,
guest star in Tiānguān;
faint yellow glimmer
first year of the Zhihe era
23 days to read by the light
mortal thoughts, unsex me here,
reddish-white omen.
Stop motion is a good example
of desperation. What you heard is true;
omens of the blood of the king,
Seven Sleepers, *so great a loss of cattle.*

ever after

oxytocin in large crowds
you're no ordinary nonconformist
espousal handshake
in all transparency
it is worth recording everything
my father says from now
yourbodymybody
underscore psycho-linguistics
yourtalkingmytalking
if we run toward the hills
tutting at airstrikes
co-dependent headlines
our shawshank husbands
happily ever after

Jewel Box

if we are a family, call us cluster

        sire a stellar embryo
    clutch in a hot muddle, an ignition
spluttering fallopian splut

I want to meet your past wives
piece you back together
undress camouflage
    drum your penumbra

wink in wink out
    who needs wisdom
when a furnace birth is misé en scene

I have loved your gurgling consciousness
    eternal cycle, transmuted murk
oh, fireballs will blaze   backs against walls

blinked out as though a chorus,
radio waves scatter   waning skeletons of light
    in long drawn-out wavelengths

    bouncing around, each family, each cluster
this one: sad jewel box, say it with a posy; orange poppy
crumpled physics

In Just One Sense

If you were also created from a one night stand,
you have my vote   chiaroscuro by collision,
where a newborn universe balanced a cauldron
of matter and anti-matter   when matter
emerges victorious, anti-matter is a housebound lover;
co-dependent, an anti-planet, whose remunerations
are redacted poems. If we decode a psi-K-short

> *K meson for antimatter: freedom fighter*
> *K meson for matter: gatekeeper*

                  lopsided matter
takes over: foreign coins in your purse, antimatter
an ephemeral ambassador, subatomic fossils
only here for a bursting moment
a twin-to-twin transfusion   *only true in one sense*
the sun isn't rising, the horizon is falling.

Reader

maybe you'd prefer post mortems;
the year we left Mum's gingham rug out
all night in the long grass,
my sister's cot-death, the meagre-
meagre breeze, my first balloon,
the divorce, my *mindless photography*
not this clarion stunt dr. persona,
who will validate my science
this pointless manifest
insofar as: have I devalued
the laws and laws, grammatical
science, the rivalry of image
as the crux

Hunters

                sweep this realm,
hypnotised by jewels, regal cat's eye
puffing out smoke-rings like knotted gas
underhand optiks   collect up cataclysm
             write an almanac, globular swatches,
central blaze, since it is Walpurgisnacht
we feel polygamous, bedded to a lacy swirl;
blue-sensitive eyes, loamy garden planets

a black eye, puffy shiner   what a cop-out
there's no such thing as chance alignments
forget abuse, or ventricle, forget asthma,
if owls hunt by sound, up here, loft and lagoon,
these guys hunt by upheaval
             hauled by the contours
give you assault, full blown furore, you blister,
you bloody human; metallurgist, mathematician,
      this is how you must heal

Pulsar

there is no room
left for me
left for My witness to all this
      My pulse is dulled

      my pulse is in the margins
carried or thrown
from person to person and this person-act
You, person, act up

It ends   in honesty   across my work

all the humans in you   out walking or worse, in here
      the *what are you good for*   is here

the garden is a recital
morning will bind us
we live the same planet out

Confounded by the loss of primary bond
Pseudo willing   I am willing
physiology submits

how you were laid down
      admit utterances
         the block of tongue which narrows us

Call me whetstone –
you cannot die in the same bed you were born

the late heavy bombardment

sultry bacteria, dropping riddles
        thunderbolts, invading
with an icy herald

a bloat and buy frolic
cancer cells queue
oh bygones be bygones

by all rights, our boys are permeating
messengers slinging out rocks
blow by blow *thwack*

    if it has been scripted;
delivering code

        second time, barely a ripple
brow, veil and suppression

lake of crisis
once he has learnt to live in an annexe
the hospice will lend us

data   data is an armada is a triumph
        is a billion figures is an equation is a junk yard
  is a radar is a sonnet is a nemesis

            is a knot is a geodesic dome
                  is a solvent
                        is an elevated antigen

Coronal Mass Ejection

Inside the sun, veil, inside my heart,
   internal forces   bleached out childhood
       beach days in the thermonuclear
compression of the convection zone
       boy, you sure are magnet, an engine
from the chromosphere, coronal rain,
filament matter lift me up like an arc
            like a bridge

magnets fight, we also fight over
who misses who, turmoil rising
solar wind, particles, ammunition
into Aurora.

Conquer national grids
conquer national headaches.

Annul my marriage, annul my gumption;
litmus paper is always at the beginning
don't you still see
magnesium burning
twenty years on
– a faint cleft-lip scar.

Origins

bearing immobile witness
      speech seeded by
colours for   priori life

losing you to Magellanic clouds
losing you to the draw-tube

      you dream of the dog bed, I dream of the nest
armoire, I dream of wooden friendships
locks mislead us, we lock and unlock

yes, the lock is a threshold
Forest love and love in a city room
anything cubic – anything which may be opened

of which does not open for just anybody
      if these rhythms are forced upon us
who is liable? this chrysalis is also mine
repeat after me, *I am safe*

      these unfired ballads

      are beyond us
the stars are locked, unlocked

Siamese

Obscure the plane
abundant conglomerate
and let's be done with it
clump   dark lane
oval haze – oval glow – ovular
profuse this
span durst   span dirge
siamese twins, siamese halo
tidal signatures
speed on luminosity
lost peninsular capes
porous iconoclasm
scintillate me Bound
we never received dead body reports
devote your *thrum thrum*
made up of whichever co-ordinate
exposure as word, as taut memory
word on word
presaging fever, whilst axioms fall
write an ode to a dead twin
written inside oranges

For Rebecca Elson

i'll still have my words

give me the penthouse, low-level plaything
abolish theorem hellsbells
in the hospice
everything is smiley

is it safe to jest

i want your parents for my parents
play harp, someone play harp or slang

non commit stupor
talky-talk-talkative

oh sky, you twat, you errant twat

everyone wants to see what is under the dress
except me, prude obedient me
thanks for the Catullus

Coma Cluster

our real drama is years past;

      floating islands, scrabbling together
in a milky anaemia, should we faint
or drape ourselves over stasis

and reignite, a final renaissance
you meet me with the dog

            the dog is a big thing to us
      less endangered

catapults love, violate the parts of me
which can't tremor   in fact, the way   to pleasure me
      is with disclosure

I am not a key player, tell me again
      how to define euphoria

you kept your aphasia under wraps
used other words

      all fontanelles are banned

assemblage

lick the gravid tide/husk/intimate testaments/fuck ennui/ posthumously overcast/vertigo experienced in the walking of it/exposed somnambulism/ebbing/prophecy like the mannequin brothers laid on my bed/baptism high junk reports/rustic narcosis/are the romantics doing anything for this lull/as if doping scandals are scandals/ample love pelts me/thermal lows/frayed hooli-hooligan/frenetic bound/swag-swag-swag you got swagger Miss

collapsus

who is responsible
for the collapse in faith
a lucky spondee
is widely used
a really enthusiastic bookseller
is two in the bush
quantum relationship
your divorce is messy
a mathematical meconium
diffracted key
in loco parentis
more trouble with myself
we hold decree absolute papers
that's me, with the Norse name
interfere with quantum waves
the car won't start
pay for bread in two shops
at the same time

Moon

how is it we posit the past
embodied in synapses
      valentine tube map
gas giants, oh, what brother sentinels protect you?
we trundle home; signal failures
stuffy intellectuals, spacial anomalies
autobiography on the fringes

perhaps we wade too far into purpose
hell, the moon was a mother
carrying everything, birthed us
by impact, oh mother, we sucked
the life out of & keep sucking

mother, you still haven't told us
the planet's motivation for us

mother, don't be an empty product
an inner voice in the heterotopia
the flux of being exactly the right fit
exactly the right conditions

I don't know what will happen
when you say *darling*
we don't celebrate the moon here

Sombrero galaxy

Wild behemoth, replete
with assemblage, leading a reaction
to spiral arms. Neat. Hats-down.
Plethora dansé: *sweet little mystery.*
Galactic four stomach throng
super black hole burning to feed

       uncertainty is centrifugal force

since equilibrium is a post-it note:
post hoc propter hoc

sweep the sky, listen to the radio

do you hear the underground emcee
dans le decoupage, insipid
relentless hiss, trace the solo dust lane
backlit, red-lit, dancing without legs:
nudie nudie nudie
       sweet rhinestone mystery.

Distant Cousins

appropriate corpse:
Mimas, haunted by the main engine

relationships cinched hue
backstreet albedo burn

seismic waves of deviance
tongue-tied miasma

winding private acts
taken too seriously

consider the ocean
an actual counterfeit route.

This July, he can not be the original
   clown around

cutting his hair, say OK
with the index finger and thumb

backlash silhouettes;
Mimas – in black milk titles.

Parents sulk,
write a thesis:

Crater Chain not included.
Call up Saturn

middle of the night
travel by ice ring.

Namely, second-born generation.
City, hit the girls. Until the sun comes out.

Merger

which came first, tearaway or teen
birth and betray formative years
as the frenzy harbours you

    Centre throng
farewell radiation
mottled quasar
sedation comes later
or not at all

heart to heart plunge
    habitable world shock
space will shake   warp
true ringdown   sing MF DOOM sing

Das Medusenhaupt

once supercilious
see this soot, discover
this impression of dust
dustdust, dust skeletons, stone-dust
new flavours tossed out concrete gorgon
gee, isn't she just the sweet flavour
of rage? override mutiny
Sicilian flag / Rubens:
maternal sexuality smacks
into the child's mind
early warning, arcane realm
open up the galaxy; mindless
immigration: fix this hot shot
stagger-then-mop-up
all the meaningless infancy

Ring Nebula

we ache to howl of her
        your arsenic arms
this year of vows
        tanked up as libertines

yet another infelicity
another *jejune* or prizewinning poem

another anorak week with you
each naked man
hasn't a place to be

what were you hiding?
live with me, fugitives

follow the save
compose me as wife; second wife
bearing witness
        á la promenade
every valentine reinforces

the place in my body

engagement ring
what a stupid world

the place in my body

        bring novice charm
rope, fresh spirit, enter here

lips in subliminal hues
the dreadful way
you come to me

the dreadful way
you come for me

birth your fable inside my throat

Solidarity

      try not to tamper
with 'alone', sketch
each comedown, note
the dust-devil colour,
sulphuric Venus rain,
the sediment
of skein, the downs,
our lapping suburban hearts
pushed to unfurl
to give something back,
how fabric life collects,
      it's not enough to just be
cradled, regrouped, jerky nervous
It's a system, a modulation spectrum
adjacent window   traffic rise

Laika

cry vapours, spacesuit clad
which dull ambush
      which project fix
is out-coded,   morse has escaped
permeating latent inhibitions
cry Laika cry, lasso each cull
thermal liturgy, the future
depends Laika, sink freedom
into bone, most loved

      so unloved
galactic bar wrinkle
for sure,
bulging immeasurable
out-flowing radiation

where should dog-lovers go
when the era chimes of exposure
      binary isn't broken
this was always the plan
always a cold disaster

Mirror

This paean or addenda;
a tiny buffered appendix,
a scarlet ibis.
Mimicry of the vastness,
think chime and parallel,
unstable universe, dyslexic cadence.
We are nothing if not fluxed,
sweltering inside our fervent atlas,
resilient, tiny villains,
bullfighters obliterating,
violence is stability,
a perfect road rage.
Else we are blanched out,
melancholic, nothing happening,
familial fractures, splinter groups,
calm little quotas, glottal paused,
philosophers on the fringes.

the interval proper to the idyll

& we find ourselves in the consciousness setting
183 nautical miles away the pictorial avant-garde,
is exploring loanwords & state-of-the-art tildes

11am in the cow fields without a hint
of phatic communion, sundowner to sundowner
i'm in for a pound, pausing too long in the street

for his pears & cunnilingus, madam versus
the flattening and thinning of life & the pyrus
alone will keep me going

Reanimate

distinguish all this from nothing
How *nothing* feels
borrowed
a thesis　　　in prayer
Hold me with apico-alveolar
which element does　or does not

where would we be
if I never listened to your stars
held hands　　in such sound
in a conforming tangled space
　　　　there is no human idiom at all

you say we are never more ourselves
than at the moment
we depart　　　　before we call out
in a non-language
and every sign a last sign
groping the walls
the body feeds from the borders
world without end

Mimicry

crude noumenon
held in suspension
    out of dubiety
out of our arms singing
no one needs apologise
Lucid in tribute
this flood, it is a flood
    :exaudi, early bird
in our catch-up
tell me we will live
gesture move this tongue
    near to teeth
forgo this   year to observe
dog-eat-dog spirals
    dust pollen
how long before we had named all this
how long before our tongue
before all tongues left by knapsack

    turned outward
befit blueprint to the swift, roaming word
fathom this, when summer rages on

    this micro scorch
of unfurling under this thread
this threat of surge
    what's uttered on the tongue
Obliged to you, obliged to be
within earshot; ear to ear, and into the limb

Sonnet

today in the grass, viscera empty
cell suicide, cell derailment;
forensics for the things unuttered
my memory is atonal, prone to chromatic
low keys, recoup the language of sorry
if neurons invite the rare
write on my birthplace
we have resisted lore
there are long months of us
I've found a house to live in
monoglottals will see us
I'm not ready for this coda
if the universe held us together
to whom do we send up our sighs?

ACKNOWLEDGEMENTS

Thank you to the editors of *Tears in the Fence, Zone Magazine, Molly Bloom,* and *Painted, Spoken* where some of these poems have previously appeared. A few of these poems were published in *Hunters,* a pamphlet from *Annexe Magazine's* Introducing Series. Some of the poems in this collection were shortlisted for the Jane Martin 2013 Poetry Prize.

Many thanks to Simon Smith and Jacob Sam-La Rose for their guidance over the past decade. Thank you to London South Bank University for the scholarship to study, and Karlien van den Beukel for her time and supervision during the writing of these poems. A special thank you to Elinor Cleghorn for her dedicated support, and Mark Lehane for his time and inspiring conversation.